Chunky Blankets Patterns

Simple Chunky Blankets Crochet

DEDICATION

Contents

Leaf Ripple Crochet Blanket

Materials:

Scissors

tapestry needle

H – 5 mm crochet hook

3 – 10.5 ball of Bernat Velvet Yarn – Frosted Pine or any bulky gauge 5 yarn (315 yd)

1 – 10.5 ball Bernat Velvet Yarn – Smokey Green or any bulky gauge 5 yarn (315 yd)

Yarn Colors

Bernat Velvet Yarn – Smokey Green

Bernat Velvet Yarn – Frosted Pine

Abbreviations – US Terms

yo – yarn over

sl – slip stitch

sc – single crochet

hdc – half double crochet stitch

2hdctog – half double crochet stitch decrease

special stitch -2 half double crochet stitch decrease– Yarn over, insert hook in specified stitch and draw up a loop; three loops on the hook, Keeping these three loops on hook, yarn over and draw up a loop in the next stitch, then draw through all 5 stitches.

You can make a larger or smaller dishtowel or a blanket by using 12 +2 chain.

Tips for Velvet Yarn

You will want to make the yarn into balls. The first skein of yarn was in 4 parts and got all tangled. It took forever to untangle it all. Also, the yarn is tied together with tiny knots so if the skein has come apart you can tie a tight tiny knot.

Practice first using a tight tension. When you change colors tie the color you are ending in a knot. The yarn tends to unravel itself.

Gauge: 5 in x 5 in = 9 rows of x 14 stitches (12.7 cm)

Approx. 36 in x 56 in (91.44 cm x 142.24 cm)

Color A – Dark Green

Chain 98

Row 1 – crochet hdc in 3 chain from hook

*Work 1 hdc in each of the next 3 ch. In the next 2 chains, 2hdctog (Yarn over, insert hook in specified stitch and draw up a loop; three loops on the hook, Keeping these three loops on hook, yarn over and draw up a loop in the next stitch, then draw through all 5 stitches). 2hdctog again in the next two chains(1 stitch). Work 1 hdc in each of the next 3 CH, then work 2 hdc in next CH, and another 2 hdc in the next chain.

Repeat from * across to the last ch. 2 hdc into that last ch. Ch 2 and turn.

Row 2: hdC in the next stitch

*Work 1 hdc in each of the next 3 ch (there is a total of 5 hdc include the turn chain). In the next two chains, 2hdctog. Then 2hdctog again in the next two chains((1 stitch). Work 1 hdc in each of the next 3 ch, then work 2 hdc in next ch, and another 2 hdc in the next chain.

Repeat from * across to the last ch. Work 2 hdc into the top of the ch 2 turning chain from the previous row. Ch 2 and turn.

Repeat row 2 for the rest of the blanket until you reach your desired length.

Color changes: 3 rows of dark green (frosted pine), 1 row light green (smokey green) End with 3 rows of dark green.

Knot and weave in ends using a tapestry needle. Cut off excess yarn. Block if you want. Enjoy

Diagonal Diamonds Woven Throw

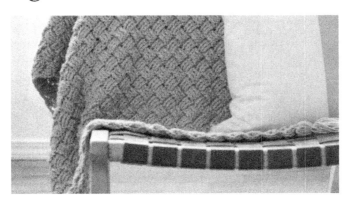

Materials:

US Size K, 6.5 mm crochet hook

7 Lion Brand Yarn Color Made Easy in Shade (200 g/skein) Kit available HERE in multiple
color options (Shade color will be back in stock soon as of Feb 13, 2020)

Pattern uses approximately 1,300 g of yarn

Scissors

Tapestry needle

Skill Level: Easy +

Size: Lapghan Size approximately 35" x 45"

Gauge: Not important for this pattern

Pattern Notes: This blanket is worked from the bottom-up with a two row repeat. You may adjust the width by chaining with a multiple of 6 + 4 extra stitches. Adjust the length by crocheting for more or fewer rows. Keep yarn needs in mind.

Abbreviations (US) & Skills:

ch – chain

sk – skip

dc – double crochet

st – stitch

sts – stitches

tr – treble

Pattern

Ch 118

Row 1 Dc in 3rd ch from hook, * sk 3 chs, 1 tr in next 3 chs. Work 1 tr in each of the 3 skipped chs from the front*; repeat from * to * across the row, dc in last ch st. Ch 2, turn.

Row 2 Dc in same st as ch 2. 1 dc in next 3 sts, *sk 3 sts, work 1 tr in next 3 sts. Work 1 tr in each of 3 skipped sts from the back*; repeat from * to * across the row until last 4 sts. 1 dc in each of last 4 sts. Ch 2, turn.

Row 3 Dc in same st as ch 2, * sk 3 sts, 1 tr in next 3 sts. Work 1 tr in each of 3 skipped sts from the front*; repeat from * to * across the row, dc in last st, ch 2, turn.

Repeat rows 2 & 3 until you've used 6 skeins of yarn or you've reached your desired length.

Tie off and weave in ends.

Tassels (optional): Using remaining yarn, cut several strands of yarn approximately 13" long. Holding them together and fold, then tie a length of yarn around the center fold. Tie another length of yarn around the upper portion of the tassel and secure. Weave in ends. Make 1-2 tassels for each corner of the blanket. Note: There are many online tutorials on how to make a tassel with yarn if you need more assistance.

Feel free to add a border of your choice with any additional yarn (optional).

HELPFUL TIPS & PHOTOS:

Consider practicing the stitch on a small swatch before beginning the blanket if you're unfamiliar with the stitches. Start with a chain in a multiple of 6 sts + 4 extra.

Below: Row 1 completed

Below: In row 2 you will work a portion of the stitches from the back. Note how the hook is behind, or at the back of the 3 tr sts to work from the back.

That's all there is to it!

Textured Velvet Blanket

Materials:

Scissors

tapestry needle

H – 5 mm crochet hook

1 – 10.5 ball of Bernat Velvet Yarn – Vapor Gray or any bulky gauge 5 yarn (315 yd)

1 – 10.5 ball Bernat Velvet Yarn – Indigo or any bulky gauge 5 yarn (315 yd)

1 – 10.5 ball Bernat Velvet Yarn – Smokey Blue or any bulky gauge 5 yarn (315 yd)

1– 10.5 ball Bernat Velvet Yarn – Softened Blue or any bulky gauge 5 yarn (315 yd)

Abbreviations – US Terms

hdc – half double crochet

fpdc– front post double crochet

bpdc– back post double crochet

front post double crochet stitch – yarn over, insert the hook behind the post from the front yo, pull up a loop, yo, pull thru 2 loops on your hook, yo, pull thru remaining two loops on your hook. For more info here, from yarnspirations.com.

back post double crochet stitch – yarn over, insert the hook over the post from the back yo, pull up a loop, yo, pull thru 2 loops on your hook, yo, pull thru remaining two loops on your hook.

Tips for Velvet Yarn

You will want to make the yarn into balls. The first skein of yarn was in 4 parts and got all tangled. It took forever to untangle it all. Also, the yarn is tied together with tiny knots so if the skein has come apart you can tie a tight tiny knot.

Practice first using a tight tension. When you change colors tie the color you are ending in a knot. The yarn tends to unravel itself.

Gauge: 5 in x 5 in = 10 rows of fpdc & bpdc x 14 stitches (12.7 cm)

Approx. 40 in x 56 in (101.6 cm x 142.24 cm)

Pattern

Chain 100

Color A – Indigo

Row 1: hdc in the 2nd chain from hook repeat until the end of the chain, chain 2 turn (98 st)

Row 2: *fpdc around the first hdc, bpdc around the 2nd hdc*, repeat *until the last hdc and hdc in the last stitch, chain 2 turn (98 st)

Row 3-11: Repeat row 2 until you have 10 rows.

On the last stitch before you change colors, wrap over with the new color and finish normally and then chain 2 with the new color and continue the pattern. Do this each time you change colors.

Color B- Softened Blue
Row 12-18: hdc until end of row, chain 2, turn.

Color C- Vapor Gray
Row 19-22: *fpdc around the first hdc, bpdc around the 2nd hdc*, repeat *until the last hdc and hdc in the last stitch, chain 2 turn.

Color B- Softened Blue
Row 23-30: hdc until end of row, chain 2, turn.

Color D- Smokey Blue
Row 31-40: *fpdc around the first hdc, bpdc around the 2nd hdc*, repeat *until the last hdc and hdc in the last stitch, chain 2 turn.

Color C- Vapor Gray
Row 41-59: hdc until end of row, chain 2, turn.

Color D- Smokey Blue
Row 60-69: *fpdc around the first hdc, bpdc around the 2nd hdc*, repeat *until the last hdc and hdc in the last stitch, chain 2 turn.

Color B- Softened Blue
Row 70-77: hdc until end of row, chain 2, turn.

Color C- Vapor Gray
Row 78-81: *fpdc around the first hdc, bpdc around the 2nd hdc*, repeat *until the last hdc and hdc in the last stitch, chain 2 turn.

Color B- Softened Blue
Row 82-88: hdc until end of row, chain 2, turn.

Color A – Indigo
Row 89-98: *fpdc around the first hdc, bpdc around the 2nd hdc*, repeat *until the last hdc and hdc in the last stitch, chain 2 turn. Last row after last hdc knot and tie off. Weave in ends.

Easy Blue Clouds Baby Blanket

Materials:

Scissors

tapestry needle

N, 9 mm crochet hook

1– 10.5 ball of Bernat Baby Blanket Yarn – Blue Dreams or any super bulky gauge 6 yarn (220 yd)

1 – 10.5 ball Bernat Baby Blanket Yarn – White or any super bulky gauge 6 yarn (220yd)

1- 10.5 ball Bernat Blanket Yarn – Twilight or any super bulky gauge 6 yarn (160 yd)

Bernat Baby Blanket Yarn – Blue Dreams

Bernat Baby Blanket Yarn – White

Bernat Blanket Yarn – Twilight

Abbreviations – US Terms

sc – single crochet

dc – double crochet

3dctog – 3 double crochet together

ch– chain

YO – yarn over

3 double crochet together stitch – YO hook insert hook into the next stitch in the row. YO and draw through the first 2 loops on the hook. YO insert our hook and draw through the loop, you should have 4 loops on your hook. YO draw through the first 2 loops only and you should have 3 loops on your hook. YO and insert hook and draw through that will give you 5 loops on your hook. YO and draw through the first 2 loops. That will leave you with 4 loops on your hook and will leave 3 have finished double crochet stitches. YO and draw through all 4 loops on the hook.

Gauge: 4.5 in x 4.5 in = 4 rows of dc x 8 dc stitches (11.43 cm)

Approx. 32 in x 38 in (81 cm x 97 cm)

Pattern

Chain 64

Color A – Blue Dreams

Row 1: dc in the 4th chain from hook repeat until the end of the chain, chain 3 turn (61 st)

Row 2: dc in the next dc repeat until the end of the chain, chain 3 turn (61 st) (chain 3 counts as the first dc in the next row)

Row 3-4: Repeat row 2 until you have 4 rows. Chain 3 on row 4 and turn. (61 st)

On the last stitch before you change colors, wrap over with the new color and finish normally and then chain with the new color and continue the pattern. Do this each time you change colors.

Color B – White

Row 5: sc in the dc,* 3dctog in next stitch, sc in next stitch*. Repeat * until the end of row. End with a sc. Chain 3, turn.

Row 6: dc in each stitch across. Chain 1, turn.

Row 7: sc in the dc,* 3dctog in next stitch, sc in next stitch*. Repeat * until the end of row. End with a sc. Chain 3, turn.

Row 8: dc in each stitch across. Chain 3, turn.

Row 9-12: repeat row 2

Row 13-16: repeat rows 5-8

Row 17-20: repeat row 2

Row 21-24: repeat rows 5-8

Row 25-28: repeat row 2

Cut and tie off. Weave in ends using a tapestry needle.

Border – Navy

Pull up a loop at any corner. dc around evenly. Do 3 dc in each corner.

2nd row chain 3. alternate fpdc and bpdc. Continue for 2 rows. Cut and tie off. Weave in ends using a tapestry needle.

Ocean Stripes Bulky Crochet Baby Blanket

Materials:

Scissors

tapestry needle

N, 9 mm crochet hook

2- 10.5 balls of Bernat Blanket Yarn in Ocean Shades or any super bulky gauge 6 yarn (approx. 440 yd)

Easy Baby Blanket PATTERN

Abbreviations – US Terms

sl – slip stitch

sc – single crochet

dc – double crochet

ch– chain

sk – skip

sp – space

scbl– single crochet in back loop only

dcbl– double crochet in back loop only

special stitch – single and double crochet in back loop only – do the single crochet like your normally would but only put the hook in the back loop (the loop the farthest away from you).

Approx. 35 in x 38 in (88 cm x 96 cm)

gauge: 4 in x 4 in = 7 stitches by 4 rows

Pattern

Chain 64

Row 1: sc in the 2nd chain from hook repeat until the end of the chain, chain 3 turn (63 st)

Row 2: dcbl in the first sc repeat until the end of the chain, chain 1 turn (63 st)

Row 3: scbl in each of the stitch across. Chain 3 and turn.

Row 4: Repeat row 2 & 3 until you have 36 rows.

Border – Row 1: Do not tie off. ch 1, turn. sc in each stitch around entire blanket. On the sides, single crochet evenly. I did 1 single crochet in the single crochet row and 3 in the double crochet row. Do 2 sc in the stitches on either side of the corner.

Row 2: sl to the first chain. ch 1, sc in each stitch around. Doing 2 sc in the stitches on either side of the corner. sl to the first sc.

Knot and weave in ends.

Gray Stripe Chunky Throw Blanket

Materials:

Scissors

tapestry needle

N, 9 mm crochet hook

3 – 10.5 ball Bernat Baby Blanket Yarn – Silver Steel or any super bulky gauge 6 yarn (660yd)

2- 10.5 ball Bernat Blanket Yarn – Dark Gray or any super bulky gauge 6 yarn (440 yd)

Silver Steel -Bernat Blanket Yarn

Dark Gray – Bernat Blanket Yarn

Pattern

Abbreviations – US Terms

sc – single crochet

dc – double crochet

ebc – even berry crochet

ch– chain

YO – yarn over

special stitch -even berry crochet – yo insert your hook into the space, yo, pull through, yo, and pull through 1 loop on the hook. Then, yo, insert your hook into the same designated space again, yo, pull through, yo, and pull through all 5 loops on the hook.

For the even berry stitch, you need a single crochet stitch between each of the even berry stitches. You also need to alternate with a row between each of the even berry rows otherwise the texture will not be on the same side.

You can make a larger or smaller blanket by using an even number +1 for the chain.

Approx. 42 in x 58 in (107 cm x 147 cm)

Color A – Silver Steel

Chain 85

Row 1: Dc in 4th chain from the end. dc in the next chain and to the end. Chain 3 turn.

Row 2: Dc in each stitch to the end. Chain 3 turn.

Row 3: Dc in each stitch to the end. Chain 1 turn. Tie off.

Color B – Dark Gray

Row 4: sc in each stitch until the end of the row. Chain 1 turn.

Row 5: sc in 1st stich, *ebc in next stitch, sc in next stitch,* End with sc. Chain 1 turn.

Row 6: sc in each stitch until the end of the row. Chain 3 turn. Tie off.
Repeat Row 2, 3 times ending with a chain 1.

Then repeat Row 4-5. Keep alternating the last 2 steps until you have 66 rows.

Ending with 3 rows of double crochet. Tie and cut off. Weave in ends using a tapestry needle. Enjoy your chunky throw blanket.

Ribbed Half Double Chunky Crochet Blanket

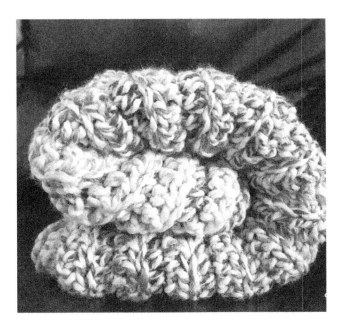

Materials:

Lion Brand Yarn Wool-Ease Thick & Quick in Hudson Bay or any super bulky 6 yarn.

Large yarn needle

Scissors

Crochet hook size N 9.00 mm

Abbreviations

CH = chain

HDC = half double crochet

HDCBL = half double crochet back loop

ST = stitch

STS = stitches

How to Make a Chunky Crochet Blanket Pattern

The blanket will be worked in HDC (Half Double Crochets) in the Back Loop (BL) of each row!

Gauge

4 inches = 8 sts x 4 rows

Notes

Baby – 520 yards of yarn

Twin – 1180 yards of yarn

Full/Queen – 1,920 yards of yarn

King – 2,430 yards of yarn

Chunky Yarn Blanket Crochet Pattern

How to Make a Chunky Blanket Pattern Steps

Pattern

Baby Blanket Pattern: (36" x 36")

Foundation Row: Ch 74

Row 1: in the second ch from the hook hdc, hdc into every ch across, turn. (72)

Row 2: ch 2, starting in the first st hdcbl, hdcbl in every st across, turn. (72)

Row 3-36: repeat row 2. (72)

Finishing: Fasten off and weave in loose ends with a yarn needle.

Twin Blanket Pattern: (39" x 75")

Foundation Row: Ch 80

Row 1: in the second ch from the hook hdc, hdc into every ch across, turn. (78)

Row 2: ch 2, starting in the first st hdcbl, hdcbl in every st across, turn. (78)

Row 3-75: repeat row 2. (78)

Finishing: Fasten off and weave in loose ends with a yarn needle.

Full/ Queen Blanket Pattern: (60" x 80")

Foundation Row: Ch 122

Row 1: in the second ch from the hook hdc, hdc into every ch across, turn. (120)

Row 2: ch 2, starting in the first st hdcbl, hdcbl in every st across, turn. (120)

Row 3-80: repeat row 2. (120)

Finishing: Fasten off and weave in loose ends with a yarn needle.

King Blanket Pattern: (76" x 80")

Foundation Row: Ch 154

Row 1: in the second ch from the hook hdc, hdc into every ch across, turn. (152)

Row 2: ch 2, starting in the first st hdcbl, hdcbl in every st across, turn. (152)

Row 3-80: repeat row 2. (152)

Finishing: Fasten off and weave in loose ends with a yarn needle.

Chunky Icelandic Crochet Blanket

Materials:

US Size P 11.5 mm Crochet Hook

6 skeins of Lion Brand Wool Ease Thick N' Quick in Fisherman or comparable super chunky yarn or 3 of the new Bonus Bundles!

Scissors

Tapestry Needle to weave in ends

Blanket Yarn

Pattern

Chain 58

Row 1 Sc in 2nd ch from hook, sc in each st across, ch 1 turn

Row 2 Sc in 1st 2 stitches, *dc in next stitch, sc in next stitch. Repeat from * across. Sc in last stitch, ch 1, turn.

Row 3 Sc in 1st stitch, *dc in next stitch, sc in next stitch. Repeat from * across row, ch 1, turn.

Row 4 – Repeat rows 2 & 3 until your blanket reaches approximately 36" wide (or until desired length)

Granite Crochet Throw Blanket

Materials:

Seven skeins of Bernat Blanket Yarn 3 of Vintage White & 4 of Dark Gray (or approx 750 yards of super bulky six yarn) (for the size shown)

12 mm crochet hook

Large yarn needle

Scissors

Abbreviations

sc – single crochet

st – stitch

ch – chain

Standard Blanket Sizes

Baby: 45 by 60 inches – Chain 66 for 120 rows

Twin: 66 by 90 inches – Chain 96 for 180 rows

Double: 80 by 90 inches – Chain 120 Ch for 180 rows

Queen: 90 by 90 to 100 inches – Chain 138 for 180 to 200 rows

King: 108 by 90 to 100 inches – Chain 162 approx: for 180 to 200 rows

Gauge

6 st(s) for every 4" & 2 rows of st(s) = 1" in height

A good way to figure out how much yarn is needed for each size is to crochet a 4 × 4 square of 6 stitches by 8 rows. After you crochet that square weigh it on a small kitchen scale. That will tell you how much yarn is in a 4 × 4 square which is 6 stitches by 8 rows. With a little math you can figure out exactly how much yarn you will need for each size listed above.

Notes

Written in US terms

Repeat each color for 14 rows

Size can be adjusted by chaining any # to achieve the desired length

Pattern

Directions are for Baby Size (See standard blanket sizes for other counts)

Foundation Row: Ch 66 with the first color (your choice)

Row 1: in the second ch from hook sc, sc in every ch across, turn. (65)

Row 2: ch 1, sc in first st, sc in every stitch across, turn. (65)

Row 3 – 13: repeat row 2 (65)

Switch to the second color

Row 14 – 27: repeat row 2 (65)

Switch to the first color

Row 28- 41: repeat row 2 (65)

Switch to the second color

Row 42 – 55: repeat row 2 (65)

Switch to the first color

Row 56 – 69: repeat row 2 (65)

Switch to the second color

Row 70 – 83: repeat row 2 (65)

Switch to the first color

Row 84 – 97: repeat row 2 (65)

Finishing

Fasten off yarn with scissors and weave in loose ends with yarn needle throughout the blanket

Bernat Moss Stitch Baby Blanket

Materials:

– Bernat Blanket Yarn in Pale Gray and White (one ball of each) – shop colors HERE at Yarnspirations.com

20% off Bernat Blanket Yarn with code RCMBERNATBLANKET20

Offer valide: August 9 to 25th

– Size K Crochet Hook

– Large Tapestry Needle

Finished Size: Approx 30 x 32 inches

Pattern

starting with gray yarn (or main color)

Chain 64, SC in second chain from hook + chain 1, skip a chain, SC + chain 1 in next chain, repeat all the way down chain (you should end on a SC), chain 1, turn

Row 2: SC in first stitch, SC + chain 1 in next chain space, SC + chain 1 in all the chain spaces from previous row, end with a SC in the last SC stitch, chain 1, turn

Row 3: SC in first stitch, SC + chain 1 in the next chain space, SC + chain 1 in all the chain spaces from previous row, when you get to the end of the row you will skip over on SC stitch and make SC in the last SC stitch, chain 1, turn

Row 4-6: repeat row 3,

Join in white yarn after row 6, chain 1, turn

Row 7-8: repeat row 3 but with white yarn

join in gray yarn after row 8, chain 1, turn

Repeat pattern making 6 rows of gray and 2 rows of white until you have 6 white stripes and 7 gray stripes.

Fasten off and weave in ends. No border needed!

I added "pom-poms" to all 4 corners just to give the blanket a nice finishing touch. These aren't traditional pom-poms because in this case I crocheted little balls instead of cutting strands to make a puff ball. When you cut the ends of bernat blanket yarn it can start to shed and fray. I wanted it to be as baby safe as possible so crocheting balls (instead of using a pom-pom maker and cutting ends) and then sewing them tightly t0 each of the 4 corners seemed like a better fit for this blanket.

Crochet Pom-Pom Balls:

(Make 4) With white yarn

Magic Ring, chain 1 and make 6 SC in ring, pull tight and join to first SC, chain 1

Round 2: 2 SC in first, SC in next two, repeat around, join, chain 1 (8 SC)

Round 3: SC Decrease, SC in next two, repeat around, join chain 1

Round 4: SC Decrease until closed, fasten off leaving a long tail to sew securely onto each corner.

(no need to stuff balls with poly-fil)

Bernat Blanket Stripes Crochet Chevron Blanket

Materials:

– Bernat Blanket Stripes in any color of your choice! Shop HERE at Yarnspirations.com. I used 1.5 balls.

– Size I (5.5mm) Crochet Hook

– Large Tapestry Needle

Finished Size: 25 inches tall x 23 inches wide

Pattern

Chain 74, 2 SC in second chain from hook (this counts as your first 3 SC), SC in next 4, now you are going to make a 3 SC Decrease (SC three stitches together), *SC in next 4, 3 SC in next, SC in next 4, 3 SC Decrease, repeat from * until the end of the chain making 3 SC in the last stitch, chain 1, turn.

Row 2: 2 SC in second stitch, SC in next 4, 3 SC Decrease, SC in next 4, 3 SC in next, repeat until end, make 3 SC in last stitch, chain 1, turn

Repeat row 2 for as long as you'd like! I made 44 rows. Let the colors in the self-striping yarn do their thing! Fasten off and weave in ends.

Add pom-poms or tassels to the ends of the chevron "v" for an extra touch!

Printed in Great Britain
by Amazon

41629735R00030